This book belongs to

_____

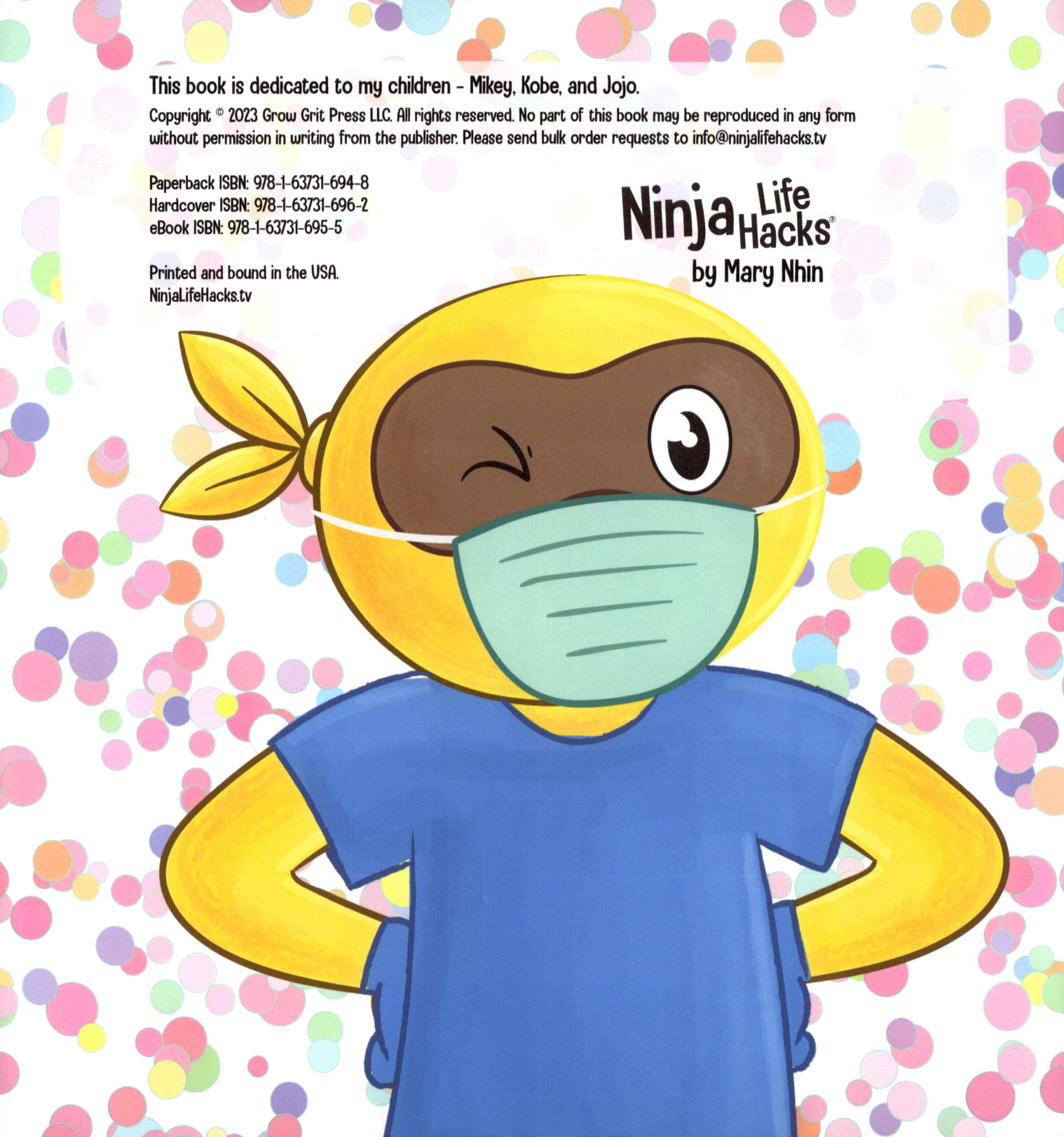

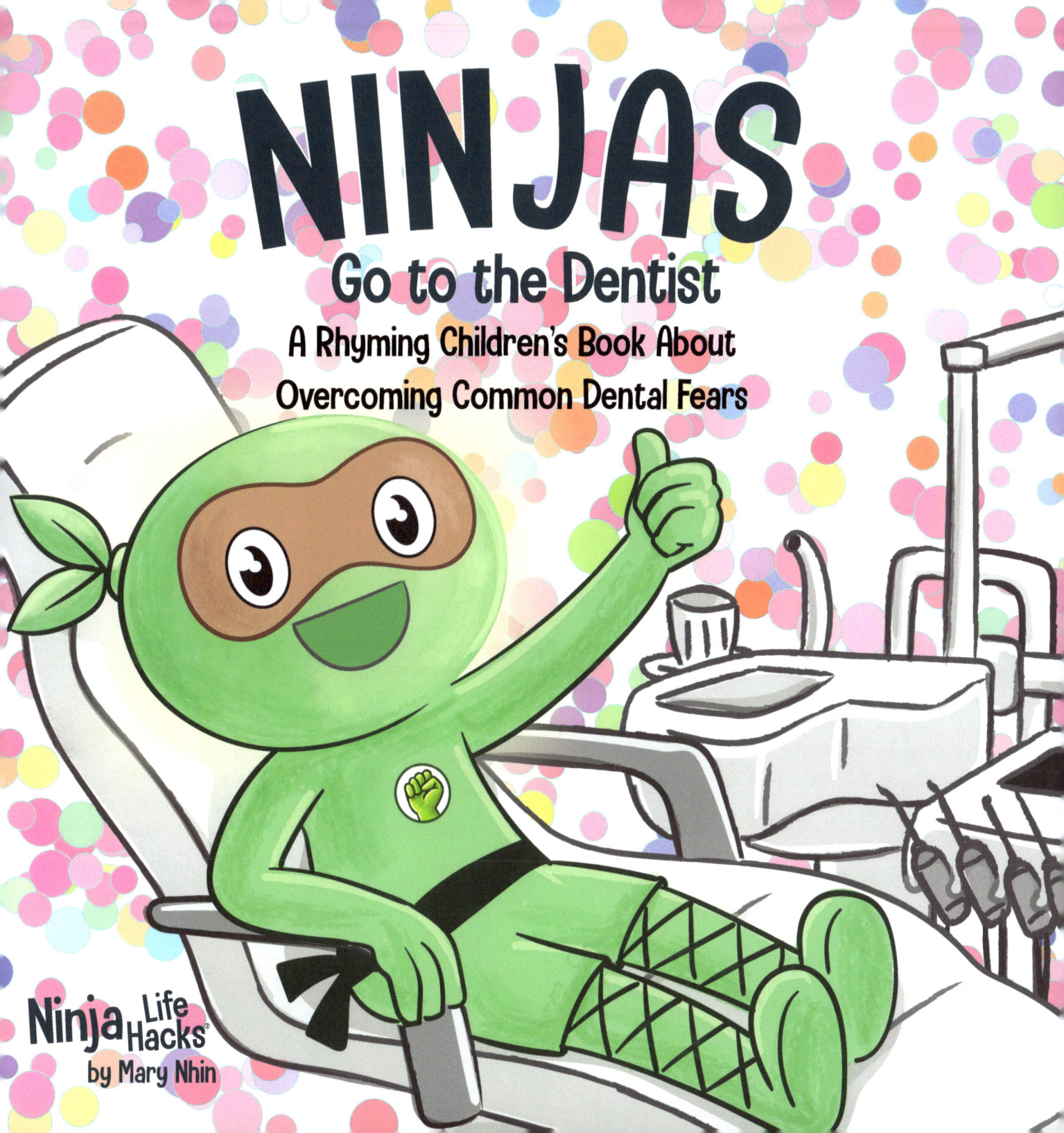

Now, I know I appear to be quite brave,
That I don't easily scare.
But I've never been to the dentist before,
I don't know what happens there!

Even though that sounded scary,
I knew being brave was a choice,
That I had to make with
My breath, body, and voice.

We took three deep breaths together,
And that was when we knew.
When we stand up tall and choose to be brave,
There's nothing we can't do!

When I saw the chair and the light in the room,
That worried me for a while.
So I closed my eyes and visualized myself,
Leaving with a bright, white smile!

Continue the learning with our fun lesson plans which include the Brave superpower skills practice, STEM activity, craft, and more!

- Instagram: @marynhin @officialninjalifehacks #NinjaLifeHacks
- YouTube: Ninja Life Hacks
- Facebook: Mary Nhin   Ninja Life Hacks
- TikTok: @officialninjalifehacks

www.ingramcontent.com/pod-product-compliance
Lightning Source LLC
Chambersburg PA
CBHW041525070526
44585CB00002B/80